VLADIMÍR HOLAN

THE FIRST TESTAMENT

VLADIMÍR HOLAN

THE FIRST TESTAMENT

TRANSLATED FROM CZECH BY
JOSEF TOMÁŠ

EDITED BY BETTY BOYD

Published 2005 by arima publishing

www.arimapublishing.com

ISBN 1-84549-047-9

© Vladimír Holan estate, c/o Aura-Pont, 2005
© Translation: Josef Tomáš, 2005
© Cover: Jan Brodský 2005

All rights reserved

This book is copyright. Subject to statutory exception and to provisions of relevant collective licensing agreements, no part of this publication may be reproduced, stored in a retrieval system, or transmitted in any form or by any means, without the prior written permission of the author.

Printed and bound in the United Kingdom

Typeset in Palatino 12/16

This book is sold subject to the conditions that it shall not, by way of trade or otherwise, be lent, re-sold, hired out, or otherwise circulated without the publisher's prior consent in any form of binding or cover other than that which it is published and without a similar condition including this condition being imposed on the subsequent purchaser.

arima publishing
ASK House, Northgate Avenue
Bury St Edmunds, Suffolk IP32 6BB
t: (+44) 01284 700321

www.arimapublishing.com

Cover

František Hudeček
Noční chodec (The Night Walker) 1944-64
Oil, sololit, 76x57cm
SGVU Litoměřice, Czech Republic

The painting on the cover, Noční chodec (The Night Walker), completed by František Hudeček (1909-1990) in 1944, was selected because it reflected the dark mood of Prague under Nazi occupation.

Hudeček was co-founder of "Skupina 42", a group of painters, writers, sculptors and theoreticians devoted to the production of modern art forms. He created many variations on the theme of "a night walker", symbolizing man's loneliness in the environment of a large city.

Holan and Hudeček knew each other well and "the night walker" can be clearly recognized in Holan's "plodding man" in *The First Testament*. Hauková, a member of the original group, wrote in 1995: "František Hudeček was a taciturn man, always deep in thought, with a special sadness in his eyes." She suggested that *he* was the epitome of "The Night Walker".

Contents

	Page
Foreword	9
Editor's Comments	11
A Dream	13
The First Testament	33

Foreword

2005 marks the centenary anniversary of the birth in Prague of Vladimir Holan (1905-1980). He was one of the great poets of his time, yet is almost unknown to the English-speaking literary world. Apart from *A Night with Hamlet* and a few other poems, nothing has been translated from his native Czech language. In the darkest part of the history of his country, he created such graphic poetry, with expressions and imagery so deep and rich, that the two apocalyptic poems in this book may be seen as a precursor to the angst of the whole world today, as it struggles with the turmoil of terrorism and aggression.

In September 1938, following the French and English allies bending under the pressure of Hitler's demands for "peace at any price", forcing the president of Czechoslovakia to resign into exile, the morale and ideals of this young nation lay in ruins. Six months later, on 15 March 1939, the German Army marched into the tattered remains of democratic Czechoslovakia, bringing, in their wake, the whole gamut of the horrors of its secret police – the dreaded *Gestapo* – who relentlessly hunted down not only the Jewish population and all anti-Nazi refugees, but also Czech patriots and politicians. Holan's friends and loved ones were arrested and sent to concentration camps. Few returned.

In April of that terrible year, Holan became emotionally and morally dedicated to write *A Dream*. He then left

Prague to travel the countryside and, during this period, he visited a woman he had loved in earlier years, vainly hoping to rejuvenate their past relationship, which had given them so much happiness and pleasure.

A Dream could be interpreted as a prologue to *The First Testament*, which took almost twelve months to write, and epitomizes the fact that "life must go on". Then, less than three years after liberation, another dark force —Communism— engulfed the country, and during the next forty years of oppression, its atmosphere of "tragic gloom" seems to echo Holan's foreboding, as his rhythm and rhyme pulsate graphically from *A Dream*.

The late Pope John Paul II, fluent in the Czech language, recited the last verse of Holan's epic poem *The First Testament* in front of millions of people in 1990, when he visited Czechoslovakia a few months after its final liberation, and these few words are particularly relevant:

> "Through ages, in vain, we invite
> peace without price...."

Josef Tomáš

Editor's Comments

Holan set himself a difficult task in these two poems, both in respect of rhyme and rhythm, perhaps to force himself not to diverge from his intended purpose to apprise the world of the physical and psychological effects of the holocaust, which he foresaw.

A Dream should have been more appropriately called *A Nightmare*, as Holan's expressive metaphors are so starkly graphic that the reader immediately becomes emotionally involved with the historic events that unfold in the poem, which commences with: *"Like a knot in a wooden coffin lurks the hard'ning moon above town"*, which sets the scene for the horror of: *"pitiless midwives are preparing their instruments of nothingness ..... and thrust in vile, abortive bones"*. Yet, despite the bleak vista of what he saw and experienced, Holan's choice of *A Dream* as the title may have been intended to inspire hope for the future.

The First Testament commences with *"morning"* and the penultimate verse begins with *"night"*, which suggests that the text may be interpreted as the Alpha and Omega of life on earth after the holocaust. The first few lines: *"It's morning ... an unsteady man plods down the lane, feeding the sparrows"* creates an image of man trying desperately to find some meaning in life, as he *plods* (hopelessly) on. Despite the "tragic gloom" overshadowing most of the poem, he makes us laugh with him, as we read such rich imagery as: *"The toasts of streets, besmeared with garlic of crowds, give out an acrid smell"*, and then, in the nineteen verses in Chapter IX, he focuses on the aspect of romance, falling in love, joie de vivre etc.

Holan may have actually contrived the title *The First Testament* in an attempt to bring into conjecture – in the minds of readers – the ambivalent parody of the biblical allegory he continually used throughout both poems.

Because the images in *A Dream* and in *The First Testament* can be so readily related to each other, it seems important that these two poems should be "married" together in one volume.

Betty Boyd

A Dream

In Memory of **Vladimír Chlebnikov**

A DREAM

Like a knot in a wooden coffin
lurks the hard'ning moon above town …
Sun rays and wind, left in the offing,
scribble, in skewed script, on the ground
about all that Heaven is forsaking,
which makes God's hand so cold and shaking,
the hand that soon begins to pour
petrol on history's new pyre
and, through magnifying glass of ire,
burns hunger, loot and bloodshed's gore.

And this scribble on the ground scripted,
the scribble that with revenge strikes,
was idly gulped, then fast vomited
by cyclists on their braying bikes,
speeding to low dives from their races
to find rest and dreams and nice faces
where, for a cheap song, one can drink
and where women are clad in tinsel,
around their necks fox furs or weasel,
and fathom whatever you think.

A bit farther, the night is falling,
barely touching, because it's blind.
One almost feels how it likes rolling
a cigarette, since, in its mind,
a touch already brings much pleasure.
And really, at one palm's measure,
it's moving now, solid and long,
having every sucking pore ready ...
It hears only what's truly shady
and thrusts within its forked tongue.

Grief, which embosses little hollows,
rushes with crowds in a tight tram ...
In all kinds of stalls, full of baubles,
in bakeries, proud of their fame,
in malt-houses of intoxication,
in sweet-shops of fasting spoliation
and, at every step that walks by,
one observes how the dead expire
and others have but one desire:
to snap their fingers and vilify.

A DREAM

Grossly enlarged, the germ of horror
crunches the blood-stream of our fear …
Without a moment's rest, so thorough
is darkness in its drive to rear
even the trees into strange figures
and lanes and cliffs and rocky pillars,
while, at the top, a bastion
pillories the belt of a river …
The shrieks of ravens – shrieks aquiver –
always eager for what's long gone,

throw black sepulchral decoration
at a stunned time that seeks in vain
inside itself a firm foundation
and mankind seeks in it the same!
Mankind that enjoys asking glumly:
what can be immortal, when it hardly
brings timeless life with youthful breath?
Mankind that grates its desire
like horse-radish – an appetiser –
on blood of wars and meat of death.

How sentimental! … Pollen, flying
to inseminate what's negative,
when flags and banners are welcoming
broken brass bands marching to meet
instincts in unanimous presentations
of mothers from defeated nations,
punished, when forced to nurse their pets.
Those instincts feel barely elated
when genitals are mutilated
(of all who got caught in their traps).

Like a knot in a wooden coffin
lurks the hard'ning moon above town …
Sun rays and wind, left in the offing,
scribble, in skewed script, on the ground
about all that Heaven is forsaking,
which makes God's hand so cold and shaking,
the hand that soon begins to pour
petrol on history's new pyre
and, through magnifying glass of ire,
burns hunger, loot and bloodshed's gore.

A DREAM

It's almost still. Calm is caressing,
or is it careless? ... No one explains.
Nations trample ... You see them racing,
after they cleaned both pans of scales –
merchants' scales from the Furies' markets ...
In clouds of flowers, nameless strumpets
count the garter-money they've earned.
Night-guards are full of circumspection,
as they spawn sperm in great reflection
of bars, and watch the evident.

On the left side of some old houses,
paltry lime trees serve tea with cream,
to relieve whooping cough that doses
a curving train, shrouded in steam,
stirred by pleas from a concerned woman:
"Tomorrow, don't light up your oven!
We hang out the washing at eight!" ...
Then, lovey-dovey silence follows
drooping eye-lids, drooping eye-brows,
with all that's supposed to be strained.

That's the moment when teenage girls
put shoe-trees in their bootikins.
List'ning to music with many swirls,
they prime their hair with little rings,
rolled on thin paper strips to dangle
like pegs, under a shining candle
and, on a clean screen of memories,
they agitate men without wonder.
Though ripe, it's hard to tear them asunder
from roots of childhood mysteries.

That's the moment when spelled out witches
and fortune-tellers go to sleep.
They drool over the finest stitches
as if they wished to get their teeth
into new planets, smelly cheeses,
godlings that alcohol appeases
under lusciously dimmed light beams …
Lips full of words will soon be melted
by little tongues, with spittle sated,
when rolled in the vale of their dreams.

A DREAM

That's the moment that enjoys kisses
on breasts of weary womenfolk,
mixing defiance with selfishness
into a thrilling double yoke,
while man is forced by the grim Reaper
the trap of thighs, on knees, to enter,
where, nerves in flames, he meets his death.
Yet, his lustful blood helps the eternal
to create, in the ephemeral,
a perfect being with purest breath.

That's the moment, at first-aid stations,
when sick men sift pulses to ghosts,
freezing them up in their creations,
monstrously simple in such voids.
Strange sounds are scraping within hearing
tubers of angst, peeled with dumb feeling,
so they don't know what darkness brings …
Who jerks their heads? Who might have promised?
As if there were, in pillows harnessed,
eagles, beating around with their wings.

Meanwhile, the town – at this late hour
always asleep – suddenly looks
as if bereft of all its dower,
when heartbreaking cries and loud hoots
quickly wear out its mundane substance.
Then, in no time, they become silenced
by a thick chignon of false hair.
What could this be? ... Some fateful sisters? ...
No! More like wine, when a glass tinkles
and coarse laughs resound from somewhere ...

Such double sounds make me quite dizzy
with all that darkened corners hide,
because who braves his fate vis-a-vis
feels defenceless on every side,
while everything else that's visible
imbues – though smartly invisible –
and sharpens, too, its knife and claw ...
Head-turning are those groans and laughter,
when your spinal cord spins thin fibre
to net and catch a winning draw.

A DREAM

Through oracle holes soughs great candour:
how to clean stains of odium;
how to plug ears with wool of thunder
and firmly close one's cranium;
how to protect the myth of semen
under the clay of verses, hidden
from all that finds no primacy
in freedom, hope, or noble action
for the living's great resurrection,
in rhythm with God's clemency …

Yet again, those tears and screaming
invite themselves closer to woes.
A while ago, the wind was easing
(wrapped up in thinly leaf-shaped folds).
Now, it grows and grows and starts drumming
on what has been and what's becoming,
and both, clad as a spectre, stay;
the spectre that is rolling, turning
funeral wreath along bald paving,
where my solitude had passed away.

What passes here before my eyesight
is brotherhood of flesh and blood ...
It cuts my despair *straight from upright,*
just like a god-conducting rod.
When (as you suspect) it's possible
that cosmos, in its pious measure,
moves directly in extremes
to the motion of human voices,
or the direction of sound traces,
despite recording all our dreams ...

Cramped chromium sparks flash from arcades
onto the march of monstrous hordes ...
Bodies, in ash and horse-hair encased,
shatter the mind with all their sorts.
The blind, the mute-deaf and the beggars;
the one-eyed, too, stay close together
with those who saved the other eye.
Then girls, who, in a winding motion,
spew from their mouths some fuzzy notion
of what, unadorned, they can spy.

A DREAM

Confined to cloak-rooms of their non-play,
the antique masks want to break out ...
And children (still plump, in the same way
as mothers are deeper than brides)
try to assist with all that's urgent,
pounding with fists into the legend
of time and space of their own fate ...
They touch back, forth and even sideways
and, having no choice for their hey-days,
eavesdrop at cruel walls and gates.

A horse, to a tombstone harnessed,
baulked in a forceful empire
and smashed it to a heap of facets,
sensing the breath of vampires
on its neck, like leeches clinging ...
It's long gone now, yet it's still bleeding ...
Even young boys are drained of blood ...
All dressed in black ... Look, nothing alters:
even the ancient witchcraft doctors
used to dress in black cloak and hood.

And the same, gloomy, dismal colour
decorates all senile men,
flung into this deserted hour
from the wet rock of their disdain.
And youngsters, too, drag their black vestments
under some obscure cat-o'-nine-tails,
the ones that destiny berates.
Their faces are pale; their eyes blinking.
In each ear-lobe they wear one earring
(the sign of serfdom in Russian states).

Cold are the sounds that join their sailing
and everyone knows what he sees:
pitiless midwives are preparing
their instruments of nothingness.
Each romps around, yet always alert
to tighten the bow of her bonnet
and thrust in vile, abortive bones …
In a short time then, you feel strongly
how the proud fruit of hope is slowly
devoured by something that bemoans.

A DREAM

And this moaning easily bewilders,
like some kind of strange mimicry …
Over-filled are seconds' sore blisters
on cracked floes of recovery,
battered by moribund feelings,
while black spots dance with deadly dealings,
till all bursts. Only those can see
who matured – despite all commotion –
and reached (without the slightest notion)
all colours of their lunacy.

The space again is turning sour
from all that packed, lemur-like crowd.
Lower than low and higher each hour,
as razor's edge drawn through soft shroud.
Deep in the cages, something clatters.
It must be short-lived, mundane matters
and even those whose ancient souls
had taken on cheap board and lodging
received short notice just this morning,
and left there only vermin ghouls.

Tambours have started demolishing
crude concepts of the sense of life.
Their hands, accustomed well to itching,
flash here and there, through a dark night,
till hot and sparkling fire-raisers
cook themselves to their deepest layers
and Easter eggs are filled with fright …
In the heart's beat, you'll find their fragments,
when spiders, from their squatting knee-bends,
prick up their hollow urge and jump.

Rickets' backs creak from slaves' poor wages,
while broken cymbals play a fugue.
Cavalry gallops from rats' cages,
stigmatizing your dreamy mood.
The smell of dead men is stamped on maggots,
so be prepared for nasal vowels
of a lemur-like foolish scheme …
In that way, bugs lose their sheath casing
and flick'ring candles start erasing,
by smoking flame, your nightmare dream.

A DREAM

An eterno-meter can never measure
when the instant slows down its speed.
From one cinema to the other,
it enjoys its enlightened skid
to where famed phantoms could discover
why unleavened lust makes men wonder
at cross-breeds of image and time …
Oh, time and image, image, language:
the poet's right to claim the wreckage
of frames without reason or rhyme.

Oh, rhyme and reason of God's shipwrecks:
little boards splashed here by His grace
as presents from His palm of secrets,
keen to learn what the Earth creates …
The woeful Earth! So woeful, woeful!
Yet, the only one and, thus, hopeful,
I want to see it for aeons …
God, do Thou see it as Thy reading,
and across it, men running, speeding
like minuscule book scorpions?

Can you see all that masquerading;
that giggling, with its brimstone laughs?
Those hearts thumping, rivets hammering
into fractured and ruined lives?
That yoke, gilded by ceremony,
that swell of lies no sewer can carry? ...
Why no girl at a switchboard wants
to connect us with our neighbour?
Not dead, but we've begun to moulder.
That's what moans in us. That's what moans.

A devil's lair turns any grotto,
or dump, or den, to surly brawls ...
Barking foxes confirm the motto
on ribbons for their funerals.
Murderous plagues at nozzles nuzzle,
wrapping the tongue in a glowing muzzle,
with promises of winsome drugs.
A drunkard spits across a railing
and, on the whetstone of wet paving,
sharpens his steps by lurching tugs.

A DREAM

Then, grimaces and enraged gestures
resuscitate with kiss of life
yells from parades of faceless creatures
that, by some giant mimes of strife,
are, in shame, to their grave-mounds driven
and then, in gloom, to high orbs risen,
to dance there in rough overalls ...
All are like grumblers, brought to spinning
by whip of homage, foaming, screaming,
then tanned by murky alcohols.

Hundreds of fingers slide in gauntlets
made of mice and moles' finest hides.
They tear the lungs of wailing currents,
as wings may do, when reaching heights.
Crowds snort and pant, their twinkles fawning,
accompanied by slanted frowning
of ghouls, passing digested winds,
till some grim nightmare, in its leggings,
dislocates knee-joints from their phrasings,
when stumbling at the stone of dreams.

Like a knot in a wooden coffin
lurks the hard'ning moon above town …
Sun rays and wind, left in the offing,
scribble, in skewed script, on the ground
about all that Heaven is forsaking,
which makes God's hand so cold and shaking,
the hand that soon begins to pour
petrol on history's new pyre
and, through magnifying glass of ire,
burns hunger, loot and bloodshed's gore.

Through oracle holes soughs great candour:
how to clean stains of odium;
how to plug ears with wool of thunder
and firmly close one's cranium;
how to protect the myth of semen
under the clay of verses, hidden
from all that finds no primacy
in freedom, hope, or noble action
for the living's great resurrection,
in rhythm with God's clemency …

(April 1939)

The First Testament

In Memory of R. M. Rilke

I

It's morning ... An unsteady man
plods down the lane, feeding the sparrows ...
He is woebegone and quite plain,
yet looks so fine, so grey, so narrow,
as one whose nights he surely spends
within a hair's-breadth of death and sadness ...
His throat, enscarfed, as if from illness,
cannot stifle the gutturalness
of sobs, his shame no longer mends;
the shame, in well knit brows, still lingered ...
The sun's first rays, that can't be hindered,
fill cavities of monuments
and claim no other ties of kindred.

It's morning ... The full moon is gone,
teasing the night: "Bite off a little!"
Roofs are slit open by an alarm horn
and boiling pots sound asthmatical
when splitting the will with a slap
of a few small words, lisping lightly ...
The apparent dead have moved slightly
and fatigued beauties pull more tightly
loosened folds of a night gown wrap,
to feel their bodies with real fusing,
while a loose breast, its tension losing,
whispers: I'd love to take a nap,
a lazy palm for a cradle using.

Then vitamins let out a yell! ...
The toasts of streets, besmeared with garlic
of crowds, give out an acrid smell.
Skimmed milk of hours appears frantic
when things – which always used to taste
of human rites, those self-evident,
facts and deeds as the most apparent –
have changed into a phantom-legend,
kneading life into useless paste
with a monstrous dream of no arousing.
Baskets feel homesick, dramatising
when banging into lifeless plates
with spoons of ante-mortem sizing.

One hears voices from diverse zones:
"That's gibberish! Look at the other –"
"Sure, you must come, so make no bones …"
"Interest? How much? Then I'd rather …"
"… should fix him with the evil eye."
"Velvet? No, no! You iron only
on the back!" – "… such a lot of dowry
and nothing left!" "Bye now, and slowly,
no need to dash." "… you may then kiss my ---,
you know what."– "It suits my complexion,
and that spot? Must be some infection."
"… and now, children, we say good-bye."
"Paper! Extra ---" "Rubbish collection

is next week!" "… from the Promised Land?"
"One pound only, or twenty shillings!
For love revival, that's well spent!"
"… cheap lemons!" – "With him? Have no dealings! …"
"You'll get fever and then, at best …"
"No, not this year! Maybe next summer."
"Hold your horses! That's a wonder!"
"Good day!–" "Stop that! Not the whole bundle!"
"And your tailor? Same as Mae West's?"
"I shop only at Shipparelli's …"
"What about slapping your ----?" – "That's Nellie's."
" You should be …" "Hi, back for the rest …?"
"And, Mummy, why …?" "For our Alice? …"

"Evening Prague! Murder …"– "Don't be cross!"
"Where is that barrel?" "Look, it's rolling!"–
_ _

And so, around and around it goes –
from big things to tiny, the whole morning –
disturbed sometimes by bus or tram,
which relishes its muddy outside,
having been licked from right to left side
by a voluptuous tongue of asphalt,
knowing full well the taste of sham.
Three houses gulped, it's now permitted
to say loudly: "Sure, I regret it!"
"We've been conned! Gosh! What a shame!"
"What? Bone?" "Look, you old guzzler, leave it!"

THE FIRST TESTAMENT

And meanwhile, that unsteady man,
who showered the birds with sweet nibbles,
is returning to his dim den
to stir up, with tears, red-eyed cinders.
So lean he is, he surely spends
his nights within a hair's-breadth of sadness …
Throat still enscarfed, as if from illness,
he can't stifle the gutturalness
of sobs, his shame no longer mends;
the shame, in badly knit brows, lingered.
The sun's late rays, which he can't hinder,
still fill the holes of monuments
and claim no other ties of kindred.

Golden roofs with abundant trees
(like tasteless spinach with a schnitzel)
show through the foggy atmosphere,
while traffic lights and gummy spittle
echo phonetic duplicates …
And somewhere else, though invisible,
diviners waddle, and their vigil
– valued a lot, or contemptible –
is perhaps that, is perhaps that
which drives the word, that hell is squeezing,
to holy heights in prayers streaming
to give us back genuine breath …

Someone is climbing up the stairs
and there, three times already, ringing.

II

Like this dawn here, there've been so many
that perhaps all are one and the same ...
I chose the one, not voluntarily,
that, out of the blue, to my door came
three times, allured by pleasing chimes
and, through frail rays, slightly diffracted,
gave me a letter ... To me directed!
And from her! Oh, so long neglected,
whom I was fond of in bygone times,
but let fade away all her features! ...
Where are they now, those doe-like gestures,
and where those telephonic lines,
I stretched to her through hilly pastures

and headphones made of cockleshells
(two curlicues with garish striping)?
Where are her dreams, in which I dwelled
as someone who's struck down by lightning
and manufactures demonite?
Where are the words, those new, those senseless,
those other words, meaningless, weightless,
and those that sometimes require less
than to slow down in their mad flight
and diverge from what seems unreal,
to make a sentence their ideal
and other words that are as right
as burning up an aircraft's fuel?

THE FIRST TESTAMENT

At one time, the mosquitoes could
transmit a plague called *alluria*.
I perceived it as black as soot,
while Mary gave off a bright aura,
and we told each other: let's strive!
Then, after we halved an apple, green
as the most precious emeraldine,
we often shared the following dream:
"When, through the globe, God drove his knife,
the equator formed ... Now we'll be able
to sail there: you, as poet-fable,
while I ... in pencil-case I'll hide
my rouge, to make laughter navigable."

What is really the time to come?
Was the future such that, already,
it *was* and we were freed from time? ...
With wireless of senses ready,
we drank arrangements of blissful words,
not aware that angelic dancing
contained thunderous news, announcing
that God had spat out their uprising
as a stone, which fell on our world,
and it's doing well, doing better ...
Beatific words, in such clatter,
cannot be heard, cannot be heard ...
They are gone! ... Gone! ... Yet, here's a letter:

III

"I'm so drenched! ... Now an ague-imp
shakes my insides with a sweet fever
of phrases, worded by a quip,
and words, which only grief can lever,
if enough full-stops can be found.
Oh, it seeks you ... Do you remember
walking through the woods in November,
you, still a boy, I, a young girl?
A train arrived with smoke and ember
from its 'collection of devil's butts'.
A station ... A ticket ... For *you* only –
then smoke again, in stripes, hence lonely.
I asked what custom meant to us,
and presence, when hope seemed so timely.

Then low clouds, the hail-makers, crushed
the very things we loved so dearly ...
Is it grief, shedding pollen dust
and, at the same time, saying clearly
that tears are a good fixative? ...
Yet, enough of that! ... Why this letter?
A more cruel cloud lets out its spatter,
so my solitude intercepts better
all that swaying and all that flick,
when someone's verse comes incognito
as your *Dream*, and pulls up a little
its mask, to show yawning fatigue,
full of infernal bones and spittle.

THE FIRST TESTAMENT

Who sends down those luminous beams,
though ardent stars have lost their brightness?
A chance? I don't believe in such schemes.
There is no chance for any chances
that joy or woe could recognize …
So far, I've been reading in past tense,
but now, with no writing implements,
I am writing, while thousands of words
are wiped off by quivering lights:
earmark your book and hear the reason
why our youth should fill your vision
of an old orchard and my house,
with colours in its magic prism!

Soon, snow starts falling, on the way ...
Three chambers are there, in the steeple ...
Then we pull out an ancient sleigh ...
Oh sleigh, oh sleigh, your loosened slipper!
I wonder if you recall those days:
I, wrapped in a cobweb of paisley,
you, as usual, in wolf's peltry,
and jet and kumiss of white frenzy,
and a horse, that jerked and then grazed,
jingled bells with oxalic timber ...
Is childhood gone? And returns never? ...
Please, come, my dear. We'll go unfazed
from poetry to knowledge, ever!"

IV

So, I am leaving my warm perch –
by displeased poltergeist evicted …
In the street, crowds, held in a cage,
are shaking bars with cries, emitted
by lustful passions, deaf and blind,
where a curved crescent of black vultures
pecks at eyes, at poppy-seed cultures …
Yet enough! … Only fast departures
bring you where arched girders unite.
A station … A ticket … Then some reading …
Ah, forget now that ingrained feeling,
as long as it stays from your mind!
Goodbye, you young, you beardless being,

you fizz of laughs, goodbye, I go!
Goodbye, all you at table seated,
while others have to sit below,
as low as the floor, desolated,
with inner armour in ruins!
Goodbye, my town, my inspiration!
Would you light your imagination
of words, as if by radiation
that carries life through gloomy years?
Time may soon have gulped enough feeling …
Yet, for me, pulse shuttles are weaving
a coat of steam, silence and leaves
and, rowdily, a myth revealing

THE FIRST TESTAMENT

that I must go to cogitate,
notwithstanding my deep grievance,
upon the verb *to devastate*:
that this is man's absolute pittance
to recall that the God of dreams
had once created him from nothing ...
As he revolts, through ruins shuffling,
a loner, his brows firmly clasping,
he's, most modestly, himself asking:
Am I the future that in me screens
the widely unknown panorama,
where there is just grief, fear and drama
of penal labour in mines of years,
where crust of death is our manna?

Yet, hear! The bell already rings …
A lamb? … No way! … A bearded monster
is rolling in with roaring screams,
shaking its mechanical structure,
like an altar boy from liturgies.
Seeing that chest, with braces fitted,
from a myth it must have drifted:
three full nights had Zeus needed
to beget such a Heracles – – –
Then in the hall, despite in tatters,
states: 'Lost and Found', in golden letters.
But rust had bitten out the first,
while only a saint can grasp the second.

V

The train was painting cows and birds,
as in metaphoric reprisal
for stamping cutlets and not words,
while a poppy field lowered its visor
and lids, like photographic plates
of dreams, through slits of eyes, so narrow,
exposed us to noumenal terror
and, in the darkness of the marrow,
developed it by tears (dry scales)
and by poisons of our feeling.
Our souls had no voice, no hearing,
before they managed to reach their cells,
in gloves of disgust their hands sealing,

the cells that can be compared well
with the wagons here: each encloses
loads of an infatuated swell
of frauds, tears, amorous narcoses,
crimes, hidden for the next year clock,
with poverty, pride, etcetera …
Walk those compartments … It is ever
the same; mature they will be never
under the sun of nerves named shock.
For us, free trips to death are arranged,
made up around, through middle deranged,
challenging it at all its stock –
and we can't manage, we can't manage …

Oh, we can't manage! No, my God!
We are only what Hell relishes,
whilst Thou – with both hands firmly crossed
on awesome chest of Absoluteness –
art waiting, waiting, motionless,
though, once the storm of uchronia.
Thou wait for what? What's Thy dilemma?
A failed poet, when euphoria
thunders with self-forgetfulness
in tragic gloom, where he retires
to hear voices through feigned wires?
But, to Thee, he makes no sense!
He spoils everything he admires.

VLADIMÍR HOLAN

He: close to Thee when he is mute,
in gondolas of sorrow shaken
by spindrift of his disrepute,
moaning that, by all, he's forsaken.
He: guest, who is and who is not,
who, for the world is Thee repaying
with screams, yet goes on with repairing,
despite the gloom that keeps returning
in hangars of his soul's blind spot,
to find and touch his ossuary ...
His hierarchy is transitory,
his despair is his tragic lot,
of which he finds full inventory ...

VI

The stations: Gladville, Emptytown,
Windcastle and Solaceminster,
we have just run through Patchington,
the train is sick of kilometres
and throws up its stomach nemesis
of smoke, pilgrims and dressed-up skiers,
whose skis are licking walls and pillars,
while you, drawn to weightier matters,
are tempted inwards for a tryst
with phantom's slang, arcane and dire,
with contrasts, cross-bred to a pyre
of some sort of strange catharsis,
now waiting to be set on fire.

They wait in vain … The train resumed
head on through lights into a tunnel
(like threading a needle, I watch bemused),
and, in my thoughts – as through a funnel –
there drifts to me, from roadside moats:
darnel, dog fennel in weedy grimness,
potted clouds, a headland in dimness,
a factory with rows of chimneys,
which stick up from thick overgrowth
like organ pipes with bronchitic throbbing …
A piece of lining from a quarry
hides naked scenes in feltless coats,
buttoned by birds, those migratory.

THE FIRST TESTAMENT

But inside, in a yellow dullness,
some heroine of opiate,
in a compartment of jam-like lushness,
was sweetening her stunning shape
so much that, under one's own shade,
one hid one's lust, with hope to render
the merciless sun of her splendour,
which glowed the most, though quite tender,
where her dense crotch hair could just be traced …
Across from her, two undercover
old men sat, shortly to discover,
with ears as to a chimney pressed,
that their passion was soot on fire.

Then there was a boy who got used
to suck his breeding like a sweet lolly ...
Not a neglected nincompoop!
No, begot in a pre-planned folly,
uniquely matching his father's genes!
He squats, between his teeth a finger,
the one, his mum calls lick-and-linger,
but, when we enter the tunnel deeper,
suddenly, he stands up and screams:
"It seems like some magic or other!"
With eyes popped out, he asks his mother:
"When are pictures going to screen?"
(So angels use a hand-torch, brother!) – –

THE FIRST TESTAMENT

And again, you are sinking down
into your mind. At first all differs
from horrors of the world, well known
to you, yet, you still pull all levers
and start, centripetally, to thump
motors of dreams, dynamos of action,
never forgetting to position
a periscope of inspiration
above the surface of daily life;
prepared to torpedo deceptive labour,
which, in laymanship, finds its favour
and, as ever, with all its might,
rejects all spiritual flavour.
- - - - - - - - - - - - - - - - - - - -

VII

The train stopped chewing its pemmican …
Look, the known church in graveyard dimness …
Co-eternally sorrow ran
into me from anonymousness
of names, and it felt, sorry to say, well!
Sorry? No! Let them go on living,
those dead, who our veins are drilling,
yet, never, never overspilling,
when filling with blood an asphodel,
for they want to spare us from stalling.
They'd love to come, when storms are boiling,
to show how white they are, how pale.
But dogs are here, and they are howling …

THE FIRST TESTAMENT

The graveyard draws the frontispiece
of what it was, when life was simple.
A pawnshop it was, so, with ease,
one used to wait, without a whimper,
for God to come and redeem all …
Yet, what we feel now, is frustration,
with graves as trap-doors to extinction,
and a puff of paganization
blows through us like sieves in a wall …
In vain, for life, we are bellowing,
glass of our own pleasures blowing,
yet, having no backbone at all …
Dogs keep on boding, nosing, howling.

They were nosing, howling at the souls –
those despondent in purgatory –
while rhythmic, speculative moulds
blurred the moon, their sole luminary,
to dwindle or proliferate …
Sweet smelled all stones … Sweet smelled the heather …
Oh, where are we, when close together?
Astonished, we say: hither, hither!
How does a tree feel, when woods feel great? …
Her house! … Curtains – wings of a flier …
To ring? … To wait? … Or, in that quagmire,
to kick down and accelerate
the pulse, which refuses to beat higher?

One brief moment more! ... Let's extend
that allurement! ... Don't let it fade away,
unless as a trembling sentiment
and as far as my will can bear
the ecstasy that never dies ...
Is she asleep at this late hour?
A lamp pours gold on a rose-climber
while some poetess – new Tsvietayeva –
captivates her with charming lines,
and the soul scrawls over her body
that it understands, grasps it fully,
but not from telegraphic signs,
dotted and dashed by me – somebody.

I almost did … No, not yet, nay!
A poplar, through its branchy thicket,
dropped to me, for some crack-brained play,
a rusty leaf, standing room ticket,
and a fence asked: "Is it valid, sir?"
A bright flash of enthusiasm
for words from angelic horizons
wanted to be more than mere spasms
of time – more than a simple air –
so it sought, with sculptor's endeavour,
some tangible tongue, which would ever
exclaim: "Oh Mary!" with some flair,
despite remaining silent. However – – –

VIII

Then, quite untainted was my dream.
Let wants of others boil the varnish.
No pebbles tapped the window screen,
the calendry stairs stayed untarnished …
Over and over, rolled the fog,
as when a bear from a fabled mountain
takes off his shoes – so self-complacent! –
and urinates in a cool fountain;
dawn's guts rumble their monologue …
Then symbols, roving identical,
and, like a poem, nonsensical,
lured me whence I have never trod,
where days may look more authentical.

One month later, or two, maybe –
after I've roamed what could be roamed,
and sensed that losses, in my grief,
gathered sufficient antidote –
I entered her welcoming house.
The corridor reverberated
in the ears of nooks, lilac scented,
and, through me, a force radiated,
so dear to all, all exiled souls.
That's the force of what's never changing,
a caress rolling, always urging
the hum of a reminiscent pulse
to turn inside out in its surging.

THE FIRST TESTAMENT

Yet now, that hum pervades no more
without sour waves, which cut a caper
by quoting what has no encore,
the never-more, with no da-capo,
that, as a child, you were allowed ...
Help can't be found in any pleasure
in women, self, or some fate-catcher,
to live somehow at one's own leisure ...
No! Who said: consciousness, said: woe!
With no pristine play, there's no meaning,
and oxygen starts disappearing
from magic flames and, in the last blow,
it dies away, as some strange dreaming.

Time was no time for such young age,
when daybreak dropped its potent spirit
and, inside us, a demiurge
was photographed as a clear image
of our pristine ignorance …
To new fashion, still unaccustomed,
ready to probe the depth it fathomed,
if adders' teeth have been unfastened,
or, in tiddlers' brains, the sea resounds …
In our youth, time didn't aspire
to measure death, with it to conspire …
And, because of that, you took the stance
of never wanting new attire.

THE FIRST TESTAMENT

You and your soul, in changing modes,
were both verbally intoxicated,
when, from the august electrodes,
the fall of Perseids scintillated
to solve the problem of nothingness!
Jasmine smelled strongly, as if coated
with sperm on walls ... The Reaper wanted
to learn how well he had been noted
in bodies, full of murkiness ...
But you, in dreams – even if walking –
were thinking about who, next morning,
feeling for the roundness of things,
the winning pebble would be throwing

and, as the fastest, wins his rounds …
There, on the walls, so full of magic,
glowed chalked outlines of Venus mounds,
mysterious and enigmatic,
each spread out like a lady's fan,
shaming us, yet still stirring our
reptilian sentiments … However,
in birds' octaves, which means much higher,
there swayed a Farman monoplane
and "stayed there for more than an hour" …
We, mostly shadows in a tower,
are *amazed* that helium can
give to someone's zeal so much power.

Then, as someone who yearns to know,
I started grasping (more than needed)
that those, who through life smoothly flow,
will never reach the deepest limit,
never, oh, never, find that end
where God tells us, in a magic moment:
"Guess, which hand is holding the poem;
the one that won't reveal its content,
if it's not, as a picture, framed?"– – –
Flow of their feelings dwindles away
and from depths, as cold as a névé,
the heart, which from a stone is made,
rises, hungrily, for long to stay …

So, that was my very first date
with the world of grown-up people.
As if armed to the teeth, they stayed,
with prejudice, which could be lethal,
though, with ownership, they merged so well
that they were seldom scared by murder,
and, even if they ate an angel,
they'd sell their faeces to a pedlar,
to make charms with a magic spell.
Are you stunned by Heracles' vision
that in the Underworld's first lesion,
man keeps only the sense of smell? – – –
_ _ _ _ _ _ _ _ _ _ _ _ _ _ _ _ _ _
Yet enough now, my hidden region,

THE FIRST TESTAMENT

enough, enough of memories!
Why should I care what's on their platens?
So poorly I hid their preciousness
that tears corroded all their contents.
My childhood, I don't wish to praise,
like some abstention from the present,
nor as the one, who, for a second,
wants, by some charm, to be seized, taken,
while his lost feeling hesitates –
I am forming the girl's spectre ...
So, I am here, but how to enter?
I have to give a cough, perhaps.
A guest at night, ruling his heart well,
yet, during daylight, with no sceptre.

IX

What?! A woman has captured me!
And how sweetly she mocks my ardour
when I make her fine hair free
from the pest of a croaking wild burr –
stubborn, as always, changed, the same!
In the library, the wind is wailing
to our toast – on grate bars playing –
while my stunned look, her eye evading,
says: "Do you recall how I was then? ...
... Still oozing the black daze of darkness,
whereas you – you, a rara avis –
had stockings, with a bit of stain
from polish, with both ankles tarnished!

THE FIRST TESTAMENT

I am and I am not … But you –
you *are*! Be it when setting the table,
or whatever else you might do.
You are the presence, simple, stable,
and living now, when still alive!"
You whisper: "Look here, at this water –
maybe less real than the author
of odes, yet, in it, all forms falter –
and here, some fruit, heavy or light
on the scales – and here, for your pleasure,
my hair – and here, my breast you treasure
so much for bringing you delight,
when intuition lost its measure!"

You, who can bring with a light hand
old patterns easily into living,
or scrub the dishes with a horsetail stem
and sway down from the shores of caffeine
a shimmy of sugar just in time;
you, alone, for almost everything,
yet such a close friend of many things.
So, a drama with a rose begins,
feeling you as a vase with a thigh!
And verse! Always glad to take a rest
under the arch of your neck! So modest
you are and yet, as full of pride
as a nun from the order of poets!
− − − − − − − − − − − − − − − − −

We walk through a grove … A light haze
tries to soothe the sap in its lisping,
and, somewhere deep, it calcinates
the insects' phonetical minting
into a calm, where a fuse breaks
at the funny bone's black-spot dancing …
Frost mixes plaster for a casting,
while ink-berries keep fantasizing
about some cool and moistened shades.
Worldly thunder seems to be easing,
fleas in an old hag's ear releasing,
and days, like stations with acrid trace,
reek of hornbeams in nostrils' creasing.

Gone is the town with all its plight,
whose folks pull chips from hats of chances
and everyone wants to draw right …
Right! How swollen are loving glances,
not knowing that all myths are bent!
Then, when pierced with a homesick needle,
they slip under, in a false glimmer,
the flat disk of a record player
and play any lie one can invent.
And no one asks: what brings the future,
or how can empty lodes be nurtured,
when he refuses all, except
tears of passion, devoid of pleasure.

All that they neither see nor grasp
they hate (because they are too timid).
It is strange that the blind don't clasp
a knife in the dark, while no limit
is set for killers on their prey!
In revolts, revolts can't be hidden,
nor, by promises, horses ridden
where God is exiled from His Eden!
As long as this world turns away
from the world beyond, it stays hollow
and any peace here cannot follow
to nurture itself on its way
to peace with death that remains fallow.

Come, my dear, come! ... Look at your cheek,
how fog is soothing all its rapture.
Your nonpareil heels are so chic,
at most an oriole makes them fluster,
a snowflake that in a void resigns ...
Lead me awhile, young apparition,
far away from my tragic mission
to feel your caress and the virtue
of the truest of God's designs ...
Let me forget the world of spasms;
it can't be relieved of its chasms
by leech traders' loud shouts and signs,
full of typhoid phantasms.

THE FIRST TESTAMENT

Let me forget for a short while
how easily illiterate horrors
can arouse phantoms in my soul.
Like an aeroplane on three motors,
they shake and wag and tangle up,
then suck and suck, and keep on sucking – – –
Come to me, greenwoods, in a hurry,
you fountains, too, clear at your margin,
filled up with tears from my lone heart!
Waft to me, wind, with exaltation –
not all lands, but just this one nation
that, as a godlike avant-guard,
reveals to all its erudition!

Did not Hörderlin once divert
as far as Asia the flow of the Rhine?
God's acts, too, flow without end
and grasp the meaning of a ruin
only by not understanding walls ...
And (as all agree) what comes later
succumbs always to an inventor,
only as a free, pristine nature
and an unlimited response ...
Why then are we for ever knotted,
into slack hearts like numbers slotted?
Yet enough! – My dear, guide me close
to anything that can't be potted!

THE FIRST TESTAMENT

Cut the film now – it's more than dark –
and name a stone, an elm, a hamlet,
a rowan, a shiny pond, a lark,
with Ascension to this aged planet,
that crushes hard the forked tongue
of our epoch, so full of demons! …
Look at ravens, how their loud sermons
are shaping clouds in mouths with venoms
sputtered through darkness, wide and long!
And down? … Is it a dirge with cymbals?
Their music steams from soups of symbols,
which, with grated bones of his mute song,
a dead man, as with ginger, seasons …

And nothing here really cares
that, next day, round the heads of children,
the ethics of a carousel
will be winding turbans, and then even
pulling up women's petticoats
above the knees of men, who garnish
their waiting by incoming darkness …
Then a gypsy ruffles her plumage
and pecks from hands of metaphors …
In her mishandled incantations,
what's black dissolves in pink impressions,
but the pattern of future hopes
returns through tubes to neural stations.

THE FIRST TESTAMENT

Another time, in reverie,
we place footsteps in an old orchard.
And Mary, keen on harmony,
says to me: "Be no iconoclast.
Look, the well, do you recognize?
Here, after we halved an apple, green
as the most precious emeraldine,
we often shared the following dream:
When, through the globe, God drove his knife –"
"– the equator appeared quite neatly!
Three sorts of sails, I hoisted quickly;
your pencil-case, with rouge inside,
changed to a cosy boat so sweetly

that the future has just become!
It was so much of it that already
it *was*, and we felt freed from time.
With wireless of senses ready,
we drank arrangements of blissful words,
not aware that angelic dancing
contained thunderous news, announcing
that God had spat out their uprising
like a stone that hit our world,
and it's doing well, doing better ...
Beatific words, in such clatter,
cannot be heard, cannot be heard.
They are gone, gone! ... " – "Sooner or later,

it's too much of them, or not enough;
just a mere image of essences,
unable to be realised,
and therefore losing all its senses!
Look, my dear boy: a tree, a holm,
and the cave of a fabled dragon,
where you, often, with great abandon,
played helicons of your dark demon.
And the coopery, a dim home,
with iron-hoops darkened in columns,
and only we knew how to announce:
! BUFFALO'S PERMANENT VELODROME
WHO ENTER MUST THEIR BODIES RENOUNCE !

There was no time – no rush, no urge –
when daybreak dropped its potent spirit
and, inside us, a demiurge
was photographed as a clear image
of our pristine ignorance.
To new fashion, still unaccustomed,
ready to probe the depth it fathomed,
if adders' teeth have been unfastened,
or, in tiddlers' brains, the sea resounds …
In our youth, time didn't aspire
to measure death, with it to conspire,
so till now, for a mortal angst,
we've never wanted new attire …

THE FIRST TESTAMENT

Nothing could stop us – no thorny fence,
when early apples were just ripening.
Thunder slammed doors in resonance
with empty halls, full of lightning,
tasting like cod's-roe of blackberries …
That caviar somehow educes
a church, where you, in twofold laces,
like acolytes, with restive faces,
were holding silver cups and dish,
and, trembling with impatience whether
a few drops of wine, or small wafer,
would be left there by a shadow-priest,
behind the altar you popped together.

And there were books, so many books,
which mutated your sap pulsation.
Laments echoed from ancient nooks,
charmed by photons of scintillation,
while a saint tarried in his wrong,
and, to soften his proud demeanour,
he pushed it hard, with monkish fervour,
under God's saddle, who, sans clamour,
on a horse's image rode along …
Wonderstruck by imagination,
we dreamt of lingual gravitation
that could propel the earth sidelong.
Oh, so total was verbalisation

in the stellar order of thoughts!
Even if loneliness keeps on growing,
a poet always plights his troth,
those, who deceive themselves, disowning.
He stays alone, but sure (or mad?)
that suffering through every moment
embosses signs without adornment
in Braille to relieve our torment,
but we, though blind, leave all unread …
Oh, my dear, is there no sun rising?
Has mystery lost its surprising?
Feel each sign on a statuette!
We want to rhyme our apprising …"

VLADIMÍR HOLAN

Was I reading? ... I do not know ...
Those moments are so full of action
that, in me, it's a constant flow
through working days of contemplation,
and that always creates heresy.
There, somewhere, I lost my vision
of you, a female apparition,
when searching for a hidden mission
till silence brought a prophecy ...
God grant my mind be not too narrow,
and space find a place with no sorrow,
so it succeeds to supersede
the Adrastos' decree of terror!
_ _ _ _ _ _ _ _ _ _ _ _ _ _ _ _

X

Frost oversalted ... Weekdays went
crystallizing into sheer facets.
The land, dry as a meal in Lent,
brought to suckers of skates poor harvest,
just trampling fish souls underfoot ...
Yet soon, next day, a few warm cuddles
of the sun milked all frozen udders,
squeezing, pulling, to test its powers
for getting porous, trickling loot ...
In unused shoes, the woods were struggling,
air condensing, on palate rubbing,
when trying to chafe itself smooth
like pellets in semolina pudding.

Though its tissue was sadly lost,
the carpet of snow kept repining
at being useful just for moths.
Yet nonetheless, the spring was coming,
with lungs full of the yelling lot,
that, for the whole week, had allowance
to cure tramp blues in their taverns …
Girls were locked in white encumbrance
by both breasts, with wedge and slot,
and threw their keys in farthest dingles …
Sleep broke toadstools of morning's twinkles,
and milk ran in a flower pot,
where a leprechaun washed his wrinkles.

THE FIRST TESTAMENT

Nothing required solid parts …
In town, they may have started stitching
eye-lashes through eye-lids of tarts,
while selling the hair of a virgin,
profiting from her stubborn whine …
Not until later (too late almost)
a gift – godsend and miraculous –
when felled in the nature of forms,
appeared unreservedly as one …
In the dark, when you feel its shudder –
sad, not free, but captive, rather –
there rose the illuminating sun
and enveloped all with warm summer.

Summer already? ... Where shades tied
vagabondage to rising thermals?
A grim neuralgia electrified,
then tore apart all originals
into berserk impermanence ...
Even the mole was in a flurry,
barefooted, so eager to bury
something in grave-mounds in a hurry
and no one said: Stop! It makes no sense! ...
And melancholy kept returning
in hangars of my soul, disturbing
with a thought that I'm just a guest,
and nothing else, but mere pretending!

THE FIRST TESTAMENT

Time, too, pretended it felt great ...
It milked the moon, then added flour
to let dough rise for a cake called 'hurt';
and, with seeds of days, at this late hour,
served it on the fog's flapping veil,
then dunked it into bromide bubbles
and pinned together sleeves of arbours
with black ribbons, to mourn disasters,
that, as fixed stars, in the heart reign ...
It hammered down the longest coffin
for trembling light, to stem its popping,
knowing well that a dying man
will always stretch, before he snuffs it.

Then a faint butterfly appeared
above a rose: the fort surrendered ...
Immeasurable was the beat
of time that pulled my goodbyes under,
just when I began to frequent
coopers' rooms, full of hoops and measures,
in search of brooches, combs, like treasures,
and hurried with them, filled with pleasure,
to Mary. I must have looked mad,
with both eyes mortified by shyness;
a statue, floating on her mildness;
happy when asked to hold her plaid
under cleared and brightened ash-trees,

when it became more cold and moist –
happy, when, sometimes, a mere habit,
a gesture, yet still, I rejoiced
when she slipped her palm in my arm-pit,
trying, casually, to spill
out of her shoe some sand or something …
How often we asked fate, demanding
to learn where we were, when still becoming,
and then, suddenly, we froze still,
stunned by the result of our action,
soon torn apart by retrogression
in two hollow forms, filled with chill
of poured metal of separation!

XI

The train splash-paints the towns and signs,
eying, in reverse, its steps forward.
In station halls, the gnats and flies
try to sink deeper a drilling bore-head,
with a promise of lewd red tone
for licking tongues and sniffing noses …
Legs wide apart, a pole proposes
to milk from lamp udders small doses
and, somewhere, a shy saxophone,
when loose shoes on bare legs has spotted,
buttons them up, each stud well knotted,
while the whistle loves to be blown,
when coal puffs out its i's white dotted.

THE FIRST TESTAMENT

On a grave-mount, a raven scrawls
on tombs and grief-yards, full of grimness …
Co-eternally sorrow blows
into me from anonymousness
of names, feeling, sorry to say, well!
Sorry? No! Let them go on living;
those dead, who our veins are drilling,
yet, never, never overspilling,
when filling with blood an asphodel,
for they want to spare us from stalling …
They'd love to come when storms are boiling
to show how white they are, how pale.
But dogs are here, and they are howling …

Graveyards have drawn the frontispiece
of what they were, when life was simple.
They were pawnshops. Therefore, with ease
one used to wait, without a whimper,
for God to come and redeem all …
Yet, what we feel now, is frustration,
with graves as trap-doors to extinction,
and a puff of paganization
blows through us like sieves in a wall …
In vain, for life, we are bellowing,
glass of our own pleasures blowing,
yet, having no backbone at all …
Dogs keep on boding, nosing, howling.

THE FIRST TESTAMENT

They are nosing, howling at the souls –
those despondent in purgatory –
while rhythmic, speculative moulds
blur the moon, their sole luminary,
to dwindle or proliferate …
Bitter are the stones; bitter the heather …
Oh, where are we, when, close together,
we helplessly call: hither, hither?
Where does a tree fall, when woods are razed?
All is Griefville, in a quagmire,
and no one knows how, in that shire,
to kick down and accelerate
the pulse, which resists to beat higher …

In rags, the times are dragging on,
as if the worth of eternity
could increase by a miser's want.
From the semantics of chastity –
wrong side out – everything's explained.
By adders' tongues of toxication,
ideologies on vacation
tauten the coils of suffocation
round the neck of an open way.
A fall, in a fierce comet cluster,
fixed the day of its own disaster,
when, needs be, it must sweep away
love – all uniting lord and master.

THE FIRST TESTAMENT

The pilgrim, once more, is filled with fear,
being seized by cellular order,
when projecting on his mind's screen
the crimes, that his days count no longer,
being saved for the next year clock,
with illness and pride, etcetera …
Walk those compartments … It is ever
the same. Mature, they will be never
under the sun of nerves named shock.
Free trips to death are for us arranged,
made up around, through middle deranged,
challenging it at all its stock –
and we can't manage, we can't manage …

Oh, we can't manage! No, my God!
Our woe is what Hell relishes
while Thou – with both hands firmly crossed
on awesome chest of Absoluteness –
art waiting, waiting, motionless,
though, once the storm of uchronia ...
Thou wait for what? What's Thy dilemma?
A failed poet, when euphoria
thunders with self-forgetfulness
in tragic gloom, where he retires
to hear voices through feigned wires?
But, to Thee, he makes no sense!
He spoils everything he admires.

THE FIRST TESTAMENT

He: close to Thee when he is mute,
when nothingness has refracted,
through work-worn tears, its azimuth,
or, when he stays here, so deserted.
He: guest, who is and who is not,
who, for the world, is Thee repaying
with screams, yet, goes on with repairing,
despite the gloom that keeps returning
in hangars of his soul's blind spot,
to find and touch his ossuary ...
His hierarchy is transitory,
his despair is his tragic lot,
of which he finds full inventory ...

Because even death itself feels
how small is the space in his verses
for its ecstatic utterings,
in which, on end, it mumbles, merges,
not being vexed by their parlance ...
Even death knows well how dogs tunnel
through a weight of stones, while we funnel
through the cosmos in our trial
to come nearer to its fixed stars.
We try in vain, only enticing,
wanting to conquer, yet compromising
the dream of fullness inside us.
God can't fit in bliss. He fits in nothing!

Man has to be completely doomed,
before he starts foretelling what is
patience … And, day by day, irresolute,
while savouring its bitter sources,
he does not know why they are there.
But even saints, in caves retired,
from their visions often desired
to learn if the Devil's throat gets tired
of the sorrow they have to bear …
But our knowledge is perverted
and, by its gloom, the world fermented –
then love, too, sinks into despair
with hearts that cannot be contented.
Never, oh never be contented …

It's night ... A man arose to seek
some hope in life, some respite, leisure.
But the crypt door leads just as deep
as man's seed reaches cosmic pleasure,
where praised non-god breaks all committals.
Knotting the knapsack means concealing ...
But don't you heed the anger reeling,
felt the least when most revealing?
And it's not, it's not his genitals,
that, with his hands, the angel covers,
when, through ascetics, shame discovers!
So dolefully his gesture tells
how, to rescue us from doom, he struggles.
In vain, in vain! Oh, in vain he struggles!

THE FIRST TESTAMENT

Through ages, in vain, we invite
peace without price to our movements
of herd-like strife ... As if we vied
for peace with no base of timeless moments...
Once, we focused on buoyancy,
the heavenly lift within us rising,
the owls nesting, beauty hiding –:
now, without seers, those spectres fright'ning,
with whom we fought from infancy,
want just *our* deeds to be lauded...
Yet, the earth itself has alluded:
Without pristine transcendency,
no work can ever be concluded.
Never, oh never, be concluded!

(1939-1940)

www.ingramcontent.com/pod-product-compliance
Ingram Content Group UK Ltd.
Pitfield, Milton Keynes, MK11 3LW, UK
UKHW041419180426
11947UKWH00007B/220